FISH

FISH

PERFECTLY PREPARED TO ENJOY EVERY DAY

This edition published in 2012
LOVE FOOD is an imprint of Parragon Books Ltd

Parragon
Queen Street House
4 Queen Street
Bath BA1 1HE, UK

www.parragon.com

ISBN: 978-1-4454-6753-5

Printed in China

Concept: Patrik Jaros & Günter Beer
Recipes and food styling: Patrik Jaros www.foodlook.com
Text: Günter Beer, Gerhard von Richthofen, Patrik Jaros, Jörg Zipprick
Photography: Günter Beer www.beerfoto.com
Photographer's assistants: Sigurd Buchberger, Aranxa Alvarez
Cook's assistants: Magnus Thelen, Johannes von Bemberg
Designed by Estudio Merino www.estudiomerino.com
Produced by Buenavista Studio s.l. www.buenavistastudio.com
The visual index is a registered design of Buenavista Studio s.l. (European Trademark Office number 000252796-001)
Project managment: trans texas publishing, Cologne
Typesetting: Nazire Ergün, Cologne

Notes for the Reader
This book uses both metric and imperial measurements. Follow the same units of measurement throughout; do not mix metric and imperial. All spoon measurements are level: teaspoons are assumed to be 5 ml, and tablespoons are assumed to be 15 ml. Unless otherwise stated, milk is assumed to be full fat, eggs and individual vegetables are medium, and pepper is freshly ground black pepper.

The times given are an approximate guide only. Preparation times differ according to the techniques used by different people and the cooking times may also vary from those given. Optional ingredients, variations or serving suggestions have not been included in the calculations.

Recipes using raw or very lightly cooked eggs should be avoided by infants, the elderly, pregnant women, convalescents and anyone suffering from an illness. Pregnant and breastfeeding women are advised to avoid eating peanuts and peanut products. Sufferers from nut allergies should be aware that some of the ready-made ingredients used in the recipes in this book may contain nuts. Always check the packaging before use.

The publisher would advise using fish and seafood from sustainable sources.

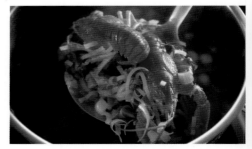

Picture acknowledgements
All photos by Günter Beer, Barcelona

Contents

Introduction

Fresh fish and seafood are tasty, versatile and exceptionally healthy foods. For example, fish is rich in valuable protein, vitamins, minerals and unsaturated fatty acids. Oily fish, such as salmon, mackerel, eel and tuna also contain so-called omega-3 fatty acids. These have a particularly positive effect on our cardiovascular system but are not produced by our own bodies, which is why nutritionists recommend that we eat freshly prepared fish at least once a week.

Many types of fish and seafood are very low in fat and are therefore an essential part of a healthy diet, especially a weight-watching diet. Moreover, most varieties of white fish, shellfish or octopus are easily digestible. Fish and seafood are valued not least of all for their exquisitely fine flavour and, for good reason, are regarded as the delicacies of the sea. Not surprisingly, they are used to prepare wonderfully tasty dishes all around the world.

This is also reflected in the choice of recipes featured in this book. From Trout Meunière and the Japanese-inspired Sesame-coated Tuna Fingers, to the Mediterranean Monkfish Medallions on a Tomato & Caper Ragout, there is something for every taste and occasion.

Fish and seafood can be served either as a starter, in the form of a soup, antipasti or salad, or as a main course, for example as a whole fish, filleted with side dishes, or as a one-pot meal.

Buying and storing fish

Fish and seafood are highly perishable, so they should be purchased freshly caught and eaten at the latest 2–3 days after being caught. Fish should always have a slightly salty aroma and never smell bad or of ammonia. A shiny, firm body with intact skin and scales, bright eyes and light pink to reddish gills are also signs of freshness. The shells of fresh shellfish should never be damaged. They should also smell fresh and of the sea and on no account have an unpleasant odour. Fresh mussels close when touched. If they do not close, are damaged or fail to open after cooking, they should be discarded at once!

Nowadays, many types of fish and seafood are frozen on board fishing vessels before being transported elsewhere. If you're not lucky enough to have a good fishmonger nearby, frozen products are your best choice. Frozen fish can be kept in the freezer for between 2–5 months, depending on the freezer type. To thaw, place the fish on a plate, cover, and leave in the refrigerator for several hours, preferably overnight. Place seafood in a bowl, cover with a cloth and leave to thaw in the refrigerator overnight. Do not refreeze once thawed. Fish and seafood should be transported in a coolbag after purchasing and, if possible, prepared on the day of purchase or within 24 hours.

Preparation

There are numerous types of fish and seafood available, just as there are numerous ways to prepare them. Smaller varieties of fish, pieces of fish, prawns and octopus rings are ideal for deep-frying. Coat in breadcrumbs first to prevent the fish becoming too dry. This keeps the flesh succulent while the coating turns crisp and golden-brown. Heat the oil to 180–190°C/350–375°F, so that the coating does not soak up too much fat and stays crisp. If you are deep-frying large quantities, do this in batches to prevent the temperature in the deep-fryer dropping and the fish becoming soggy and unappetizing.

Whole fish, fillets and shellfish can also be shallow-fried in a frying pan. Before frying, coat the fish in flour. Again, make sure the fat in the pan is hot enough before adding the fish, and avoid overcrowding. Fry fillets on the skin side first, and then briefly on the flesh side.

This ensures that the skin becomes crispy and the flesh remains succulent and full of flavour.

Fish and shellfish can also be cooked in liquid. However, fish should not be left to simmer too long because it falls apart easily, while shellfish tends to become tough if overcooked. A wonderful way to cook whole fish and shellfish in liquid is to poach them in stock, wine or water. Remember to keep the liquid below boiling point to prevent the fish falling apart while cooking.

Whole and stuffed fish, fish fillets and steaks, as well as shellfish, can also be oven-baked. A little liquid, oil or melted butter is poured over the fish to prevent it drying out. The fish can also be covered with a lid, foil or a salty crust. A particularly low-fat method of preparing fish is to steam it. The fish is placed on a steamer tray over a saucepan of boiling liquid and allowed to cook gently. This method of cooking also preserves valuable nutrients.

In the summer, of course, fish and shellfish can also be barbecued. For an exceptionally tasty result, simply brush the fish with oil mixed with lemon juice and herbs. This is a quick and easy way to prepare delicious fish and shrimp brochettes as well as whole fish. However, whole fish or pieces of fish should not be more than 5 cm/ 2 inches thick, otherwise they will not cook through properly.

With fresh fish and shellfish, you can treat yourself, your family and friends to a wide variety of healthy and highly nutritious dishes that are simple to prepare and delicious to eat.

How to use this book

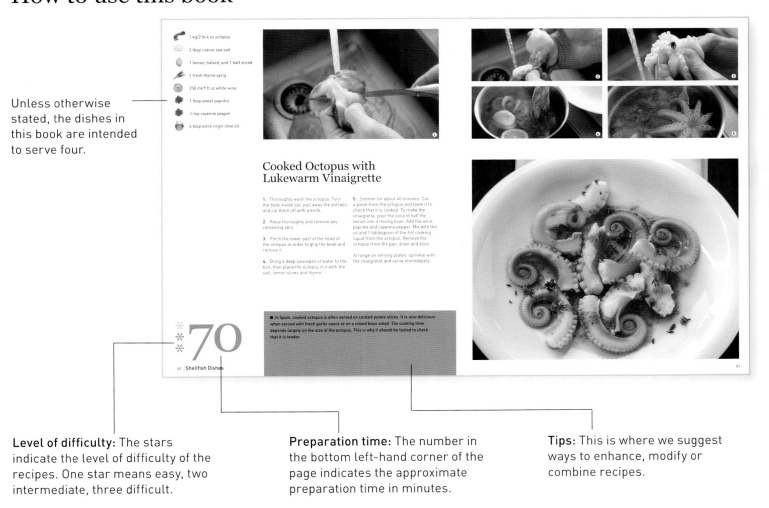

Unless otherwise stated, the dishes in this book are intended to serve four.

Level of difficulty: The stars indicate the level of difficulty of the recipes. One star means easy, two intermediate, three difficult.

Preparation time: The number in the bottom left-hand corner of the page indicates the approximate preparation time in minutes.

Tips: This is where we suggest ways to enhance, modify or combine recipes.

Cleaning & Descaling Fish

Ask your fishmonger to gut the fish and cut the gills before you take it home.

Use sharp kitchen scissors to cut off the pectoral fins.

Cut off the pelvic fins with scissors.

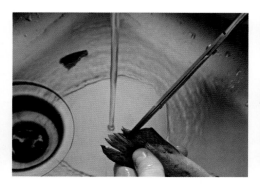

Trim the tail fin by half, otherwise it could burn during pan-frying.

Use a small kitchen knife to scale the fish.

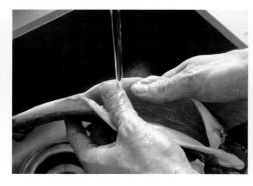

Rinse well under running water and wash off any blood and pieces of skin.

If you descale the fish under running water, the scales will be rinsed off by the water rather than flying all over the kitchen.

Remove the excess water by hand.

Place the fish on kitchen paper and make a small slit in the skin from the head to the tail fin. It is easier to get the knife under the flesh to fillet the fish this way, and it prevents the skin tearing irregularly during frying.

How to Fillet Fish

Place the fish on a chopping board to fillet it.

Using a knife, cut at an angle from the head to the backbone.

Turn the blade towards the tail fin and make a small cut.

Push the knife along the backbone and cut off the fillet. Ensure that the top fillet is always stretched as this makes the job easier. Remove the fillet with the knife all the way to the tail fin. Turn the fish over and remove the bottom fillet.

Remove the rib cage without cutting away too much flesh and put the cuttings aside.

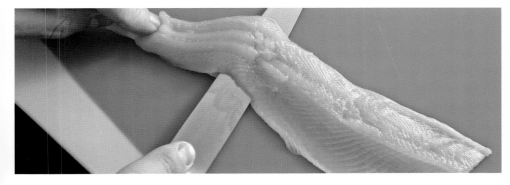

Separate the fillet from the skin. Hold the skin with one hand and, with your other hand, remove the fillet using the knife.

Remove the small bones with fish pliers.

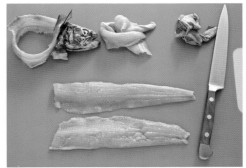

The leftovers from filleting can be used to prepare fish stock later. Stock from freshwater fish is sometimes a bit cloudy and does not have the distinctive taste of saltwater fish stock.

1 bunch fresh dill

 3 cucumbers

 800 g/1 lb 12 oz salmon fillets, skinned

 ½ horseradish root, grated

 1 lemon

 60 g/2¼ oz butter

 salt and white pepper

 pinch of sugar

 200 ml/7 fl oz fish stock

 100 ml/3½ fl oz double cream

 100 ml/3½ fl oz crème fraîche

2 tbsp double cream, whipped

1

Salmon Fillets with Horseradish Butter & Dill Pickles

1. Wash the dill and set it aside. Peel the cucumbers, halve them lengthways and remove the seeds with a small spoon. Cut the cucumbers diagonally into 1-cm/½-inch thick slices.

2. Skin and clean the salmon, remove any bones with fish pliers, and cut the fillets into 4 equal portions. Marinate the fillets with the horseradish and the juice of half the lemon. Cut the other half lemon into thin slices.

3. Melt 20 g/⅔ oz of the butter in a wide saucepan over a medium heat and add the cucumber slices. Season with salt and pepper, add the sugar, and sauté briefly. Add the stock and simmer for about 5 minutes until it is reduced by half.

4. Add the cream and the crème fraîche and simmer for 1 minute. Finely chop the dill, mix with the whipped cream, then add the mixture to the cucumbers.

5. In the meantime, melt the remaining butter in a non-stick frying pan. Season the marinated salmon steaks and place in the pan. Slowly sauté on both sides for about 3 minutes, while pouring the butter from the pan over.

Arrange the cooked cucumbers on plates, place a piece of salmon on each plate and garnish with a slice of lemon.

■ You can prepare a horseradish crust for the salmon pieces by beating 60 g/2¼ oz butter until creamy, then adding 2 egg yolks, 2 tablespoons of grated horseradish and 80 g/2¾ oz of white breadcrumbs. Mix the ingredients and season to taste with salt and pepper. Pour the mixture over the raw salmon pieces and place them in a buttered soufflé dish. Pour over 100 ml/3½ fl oz of white wine and bake for 15 minutes at 180°C/350°F/Gas Mark 4 until golden brown.

150 g/5½ oz butter, plus extra for greasing

 large bunch fresh dill

 bunch fresh parsley

 1 egg yolk

 salt and white pepper

 2 tbsp breadcrumbs

 4 salmon fillets, 200 g/7 oz each, skinned

 100 ml/3½ fl oz dry white wine

 1 lemon

Slow Roast Salmon

1. Preheat the oven to 110°C/225°F/Gas Mark ¼. Put the butter in a small mixing bowl and beat until creamy. Finely chop the dill and the parsley. Separate the egg white from the yolk and mix the yolk with the butter and the herbs. Season to taste with salt and pepper. Carefully mix in the breadcrumbs and season to taste again.

2. Grease a soufflé dish. Season the salmon portions with salt, place them in the prepared dish, and brush on the herb butter.

3. Pour the wine over the fish. Slice the lemon and add 1 slice to each portion.

4. Cook the salmon in the preheated oven for 30–35 minutes.

Remove from the oven and serve with white bread.

■ Vary this salmon dish by chopping the herbs together with 1 tablespoon of ginger and 1 bunch of fresh coriander and adding the butter. Then continue as described above.

4 trout, 250 g/9 oz each

 salt

 flour, for dusting

 4 tbsp vegetable oil

 80 g/2¾ oz butter

 bunch fresh parsley, finely chopped

 juice of 1 lemon

* * * 35

Trout Meunière

1. Gut the trout and descale, clean and drain them. Season the fish inside and outside with salt and dust them lightly with flour.

2. Heat the oil in an oval frying pan; place the trout in the pan and cook for about 5–7 minutes on each side. When each trout is golden brown in colour on both sides, remove the oil from the pan using a tablespoon.

3. Add the butter to the pan, sprinkle over the parsley and sauté the fish. Add the lemon juice to the pan, then transfer the fish to a serving dish, and serve immediately.

 4 trout, 250 g/9 oz each

 salt

 flour, for dusting

 4 tbsp vegetable oil

 80 g/2¾ oz butter

 60 g/2¼ oz flaked almonds

 juice of 1 lemon

* * * 35

Trout Amandine

1. Gut the trout and descale, clean and drain them. Season the fish inside and outside with salt and dust them lightly with flour.

2. Heat the oil in an oval frying pan; place the trout in the pan and cook for about 5–7 minutes on each side. When each trout is golden brown in colour on both sides, remove the oil from the pan using a tablespoon.

3. Add the butter and the flaked almonds to the pan and sauté. The almonds should be light golden brown in colour. Add the lemon juice, transfer the fish to a serving dish and serve immediately.

250 ml/9 fl oz red wine

 100 ml/3½ fl oz port

 pinch of sugar

 150 ml/5 fl oz double cream

 salt and pepper

 100 g/3½ oz butter

 400 g/14 oz fresh spinach

 freshly grated nutmeg

 4 John Dory fillets, 140–160 g/ 5–5¾ oz each

 juice of ½ lemon

 2 tbsp vegetable oil

 8 fresh lemon thyme sprigs

Poached John Dory in a Red Wine & Butter Sauce

1. Combine the wine and port with the sugar in a saucepan, bring to the boil and cook until the liquid has reduced to about a sixth of its volume.

2. Add 3½ tablespoons of the cream and bring to the boil. Season to taste with salt and pepper.

3. Cut 60 g/2¼ oz of the butter into thin slices and place in the wine reduction to bind it. Set the sauce aside.

4. Melt 20 g/⅔oz of the butter in a saucepan until it foams, add the spinach leaves and leave them to sweat. Season with salt and pepper and nutmeg to taste. Add the remaining cream and slowly simmer for a further 2 minutes.

5. Using a kitchen knife, cut the fish fillets into nice shapes, sprinkle the lemon juice over them and season with salt on both sides. Heat the remaining butter and the oil in a non-stick saucepan. Place the fillets in the pan and top each with a sprig of lemon thyme. Pour some butter over the fish occasionally and slowly sauté for about 3 minutes on each side until they are lightly coloured.

Arrange some spinach in the middle of four plates and carefully pour the reserved sauce around; place a fish fillet on top and garnish with lemon thyme.

■ A good-quality red wine is an absolute must for a flavourful red wine and butter sauce. This recipe can also be prepared using turbot, haddock, flounder or pike instead of the John Dory. Leeks or chard can be substituted for the spinach.

4 catfish fillets, 140–160 g/ 5–5¾ oz each, skinned

 80 g/2¾ oz leeks

 80 g/2¾ oz carrots

 ¼ head celeriac

 750 ml/1¼ pints water

 salt

 3 tbsp white wine vinegar or cider vinegar

 1 onion

 1 bay leaf

 1 clove

 150 ml/5 fl oz fish stock

 50 g/1¾ oz cold butter

 small bunch fresh chives

 ½ horseradish root, grated

① ② ③

Catfish in Root Vegetable Stock

1. Using a knife, trim the catfish fillets and cut them in half. Slice the leeks, carrots and celeriac into long thin strips. Put the water into a large saucepan with 2 tablespoons of salt and the vinegar. Stud the onion with the bay leaf and clove, and place it in the pan. Bring to the boil and simmer for 5 minutes. Place the catfish in this stock, remove from the heat and leave to stand for 8–10 minutes. Meanwhile, bring a saucepan of lightly salted water to the boil, add the vegetable strips, bring back to the boil and cook for about 1 minute, then refresh the vegetables in cold water.

2. Combine the fish stock with 200 ml/ 7 fl oz of the cooking stock, strain into a saucepan, bring to the boil and cook for 5 minutes to reduce the liquid. Add the butter, using a wire whisk to blend the stock more easily. Finely chop the chives.

3. Place the julienned vegetables and the catfish fillets in the stock and bring to the boil. Serve in soup bowls, garnished with the chives and horseradish.

■ **Cod fillets can be prepared in the same way. However, increase the cooking time to 8 minutes and add 1 teaspoon of mustard to the stock for extra flavour.**

45

1

2

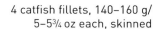
4 catfish fillets, 140–160 g/
5–5¾ oz each, skinned

juice of 1 lemon

salt and white pepper

sweet paprika

1 tbsp extra virgin olive oil

750 ml/1¼ pints Paprika
Cream Sauce (see left)

2 tbsp double cream, whipped

Catfish in Paprika Sauce

Using a knife, trim the skinned catfish
fillets and cut into 2-cm/¾-inch strips.
Place in a bowl and sprinkle with the
lemon juice. Season to taste with salt and
pepper and paprika. Add the oil and mix.
Marinate for about 10 minutes.

Pour the paprika cream sauce into a
saucepan and bring to the boil. Place the
marinated strips of catfish in the sauce
and reheat slowly for about 3 minutes. Do
not allow to boil, because this will make
the fish tough.

Mix in the whipped cream and arrange on
plates to serve.

■ To make the Paprika Cream Sauce,
dice 500 g/1 lb 2 oz of red peppers. Thinly
slice 1 onion and 2 garlic cloves. Heat
4 tablespoons of extra virgin olive oil in a
saucepan, add the onion and garlic and
sweat until translucent. Add 1 thyme
sprig, 2 bay leaves and the red pepper,
then add 1 tablespoons of sugar and
season with salt and pepper. Pour in
150 ml/5 fl oz of white wine and about
600 ml/1 pint of chicken stock and simmer
for about 15 minutes. Remove the herbs
and mix the sauce with a hand-held
blender. Pass the mixture through a fine
sieve, pressing the vegetables through so
that the sauce is rich and thick.

20

2 carp fillets

 1 pinch of salt
1 pinch of black pepper

 2 lemons

 2 eggs

 100 g/3½ oz flour

 500 g/1 lb 2 oz breadcrumbs

 4 tbsp oil

 60 g/2¼ oz butter

Carp Fried in Batter

1. Descale the carp fillets and clean with kitchen paper. Hold the fish with one hand while carefully removing the bones with fish pliers.

2. Cut the fillets into 3-cm/1¼-inch wide strips and feel with your fingers for any remaining bones. If necessary, use the fish pliers again.

3. Season the carp strips with the salt and pepper. Halve 1 of the lemons and rub the fish on both sides with a lemon half. Slice the other lemon into small wedges and reserve as a garnish.

4. Beat the eggs in a shallow dish. Spread the flour on the base of a separate shallow dish and put the breadcrumbs in a dish or plate. Dip the carp strips into the flour to coat both sides, then dip them in the egg mixture. Dip in the breadcrumbs to coat and gently pat the batter in place.

5. Melt the oil and butter in a large frying pan, add the carp pieces and fry on both sides for about 8 minutes until golden brown.

Place on kitchen paper to drain, then serve with the lemon wedges and a potato and vegetable salad.

■ Carp is predominantly used in 'gefilte fish', or stuffed fish, which is a traditional Jewish dish. If you use a large carp, remove the skin with a long sharp kitchen knife to avoid the dish becoming too fatty. It is best to use a carp approximately 1–1.5 kg/2 lb 4 oz–3 lb 5 oz in weight.

1 aubergine

 salt

 6 tbsp extra virgin olive oil

 1 tsp tandoori powder

 2 red onions, finely chopped

 3 tomatoes, peeled and diced

 10 fresh basil leaves, chopped

 2.5-cm/1-inch piece fresh ginger, peeled and finely grated

 4 limes

 pepper

 800 g/1 lb 12 oz tuna fillet

Tuna Steaks

1. Cut the aubergine into 1-cm/½-inch thick slices and season to taste with salt. Add 2 tablespoons of the oil to a frying pan, add the aubergine slices and sauté on both sides. Mix the tandoori powder with 2 tablespoons of the oil in a small bowl and lightly season with salt.

2. Combine the onions, tomatoes, basil and ginger in a bowl with the juice of 2 of the limes. Season to taste with salt and pepper.

3. Cut the tuna fillet into 3-cm/1¼-inch thick steaks, spread the remaining oil over them and season to taste with salt. Cut the 2 remaining limes in half.

4. Heat a non-stick griddle pan, add the tuna steaks and cook for 2 minutes on each side.

Divide the tomato-onion mixture between four serving plates and arrange the fried aubergine slices and tuna steaks over it. Garnish with the tandoori oil and lime halves and serve.

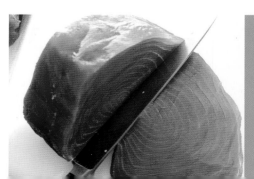

■ Tuna remains fresh for longer if sliced shortly before cooking.

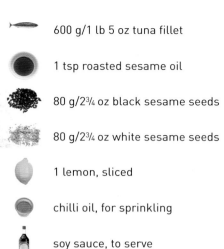

- 600 g/1 lb 5 oz tuna fillet
- 1 tsp roasted sesame oil
- 80 g/2¾ oz black sesame seeds
- 80 g/2¾ oz white sesame seeds
- 1 lemon, sliced
- chilli oil, for sprinkling
- soy sauce, to serve

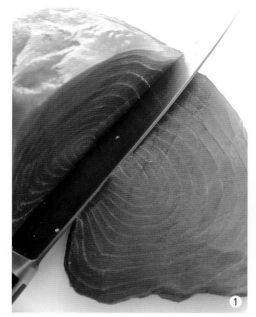

Sesame-coated Tuna Fingers

1. Pat dry the tuna fillet, remove any tendons, and cut into 1-cm/½-inch thick slices.

2. Cut the slices into 2-cm/¾-inch thick strips.

3. Sprinkle the roasted sesame oil over the strips and turn them so that they are evenly coated.

4. Place the tuna pieces on a tray with the mixed black and white sesame seeds, turning the fish over to coat them on all sides with the seeds.

5. Put the fish in a non-stick frying pan and fry without oil for about 1 minute. The tuna should be slightly raw on the inside. If you prefer it well done double the cooking time.

Arrange the fish fingers on a serving plate, add the lemon slices, sprinkle a little chilli oil over and serve with soy sauce.

15

■ The sesame seeds can be mixed with chopped fennel seeds, coriander seeds or a few Szechuan peppercorns. This will give the tuna fingers more zest and aroma.

2 shallots

 750 g/1 lb 10 oz cherry tomatoes of various colours

 1 tbsp capers

 1 garlic clove

 small bunch fresh basil

 1.5 kg/3 lb 5 oz monkfish tail

 1 fresh thyme sprig

 30 g/1 oz butter

 2 tbsp extra virgin olive oil

 salt

 sugar

 pepper

 500 ml/18 fl oz fish stock

 2 tbsp sunflower oil

 sea salt

 1 tbsp coarse mustard

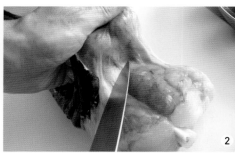

Monkfish Medallions on a Tomato & Caper Ragout

1. Dice the shallots. Peel the tomatoes. Chop the capers. Peel and dice the garlic. Chop the basil into fine strips.

2. Prepare the monkfish. First, remove the outer skin by holding it taut with your left hand and cutting it with the tip of a sharp knife. Pull off the last 10 cm/ 4 inches of the skin with your fingers.

3. Use scissors to cut off the dorsal and ventral fins.

4. Carefully remove the top layer of the skin and all the bloody skin layers with a sharp knife. Cut the fish into 3-cm/ 1¼-inch thick slices.

5. Pluck the thyme leaves off the stalks and sprinkle over the monkfish.

6. Melt one third of the butter with the olive oil in a saucepan over a medium heat, add the garlic and shallots and brown. Add the tomatoes and season to taste with salt and pepper and nutmeg. Reduce the temperature to low. Pour in the stock and add sea salt to taste, stir in the mustard and simmer for 7 minutes.

■ The range of tomatoes adds a variety of both colour and flavour to the ragout.

50

7. Pour the sunflower oil into a frying pan, add the the monkfish and sauté on each side for 2–3 minutes over a medium–high heat. Season with sea salt.

8. Add the capers, basil and the remaining butter to the tomatoes and lightly toss in the pan.

Arrange the finished tomato ragout on serving plates, place the monkfish on top and serve immediately.

3 eggs

 300 g/10½ oz plain flour

 1 tsp baking powder

 salt

 360 ml/12½ fl oz beer

 600 g/1 lb 5 oz salmon fillet

 white pepper

 juice of ½ lemon

 2 litres/3½ pints vegetable oil, for frying

Salmon in Beer Batter

1. Separate the eggs and refrigerate the egg whites. Pour the flour into a mixing bowl. Add the egg yolks, baking powder and a pinch of salt.

2. Gradually add the beer, beating until the batter is smooth.

3. Add some vegetable oil to the batter. Beat the egg whites with a pinch of salt until holding soft peaks, and carefully fold into the batter.

4. Cut the salmon fillets into 40-g/1½-oz pieces, season with salt and pepper, sprinkle some lemon juice over them and carefully dip them in the batter.

5. Meanwhile heat the oil in a large saucepan to 160°C/325°F. Add the salmon and fry for about 5 minutes, then turn. Drain on kitchen paper.

Serve immediately, with lemon wedges for squeezing over.

■ To prevent the fat splattering, it is best to use a high-sided saucepan.

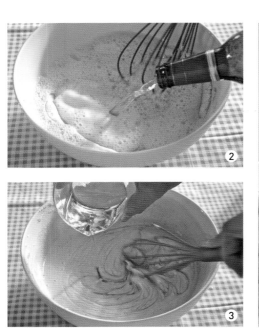

½ leek

 5 button mushrooms

 40 g/1½ oz butter

 4 bream fillets, 180 g/6 oz each

 salt

 white pepper

 40 ml/1½ fl oz vermouth

 150 ml/5 fl oz white wine

 1 tbsp fresh basil leaves

Sautéed Bream Fillets in White Wine with Button Mushrooms

1. Cut the leek in half lengthways and slice into thin strips. Thinly slice the mushrooms. Heat 2 tablespoons of the butter in a frying pan until foaming, then add the leek and mushrooms and season with a little salt.

2. Pat the bream fillets dry with kitchen paper and season with salt and pepper. Put the fish on top of the vegetables in the pan.

3. Add the vermouth and wine and reduce the heat by about two thirds.

4. Sprinkle with the basil leaves, cover and steam for about 5 minutes, then add the remaining cold butter.

Serve immediately with potatoes or rice.

■ Try this dish with sea bass, turbot or halibut fillets instead of the bream and serve with butter sauce.

2 kg/4 lb 8 oz coarse sea salt

 1 bream, about 1 kg/2 lb 4 oz, unscaled

 1 fennel slice

 1 lime slice

 10 white peppercorns

 1 fresh rosemary sprig

 fennel greens

Bream Baked in a Salt Crust

1. Preheat the oven to 230°C/450°F/ Gas Mark 8. Moisten the salt with a little water and mix.

2. Fill the prepared bream with the fennel slice, lime slice, peppercorns, rosemary and fennel greens. Then close the fish up, so that no salt crust can get inside the fish.

3. Place some baking paper on a baking tray and add a 1-cm/½-inch layer of the damp salt. Place the bream on top and cover with the remaining salt.

4. Pat down the salt around the fish to form the shape of a fish.

5. Put the fish in the preheated oven and cook for about 35 minutes. Break open the salt crust and remove the fish.

6. Cut the skin along the backbone, and then use a spoon and a knife to skin the fish.

7. Carefully remove the fillets, ensuring that the fish does not come into contact with the salt crust.

Place the fillets on a serving plate and reassemble them. Serve with fresh bread or rosemary potatoes.

■ Prepare a light vinaigrette using diced tomatoes, olive oil, lemon juice, fennel greens and salt and pepper, and drizzle it over the fish fillets.

2 sole

 salt

 200 g/7 oz white fish fillet, such as cod

 50 ml/2 fl oz double cream

 cayenne pepper

 bunch fresh flat-leaf parsley, plus extra sprigs to garnish

 10 fresh basil leaves

 2 fresh tarragon sprigs

 small bunch fresh chives

 300 g/10½ oz potatoes

150 ml/5 fl oz Clarified Butter (see below)

Stuffed Sole Garnished with Potato Scales

1. Use a sharp flexible knife to cut the prepared sole along their backbones. Slowly loosen the fillet until the centre bone is clearly visible, but the fillets are still attached to the sole.

2. Using kitchen scissors, separate the outside of the centre bone, starting from the tail.

3. Using the knife, cut along the centre bone to loosen it.

4. Bend the centre bone, which is now only attached at one point, from the tail end up and gradually pull out. Season the sole on the inside and outside with salt.

5. Cut the white fish fillet into cubes and place in the freezer for 5 minutes. Place the chilled fish cubes in a food processor, add the cream and mix until smooth. Season with salt and cayenne pepper. Finely chop the parsley, basil, tarragon and chives and add to the mixture. Spread the filling on the open sole.

6. Close the fillets. This brings the sole back to their original shape.

7. Peel the potatoes and slice paper thin. Place 3 slices on top of each other and cut out 2-cm/¾-inch circles.

■ To make Clarified Butter, put the butter in a saucepan over a low heat and gently melt. Skim off any froth that appears on the surface – this will reveal a clear yellow layer on top of a milky layer. Pour the clear fat into a bowl or jug, discarding the milky residue. Clarified butter will keep in the refrigerator for several weeks and can be frozen for longer.

8. Place the potato slices in a scale-like pattern on the sole, generously brush on the clarified butter, then season with salt.

9. Place the sole in the freezer for 3 minutes, so the butter solidifies and the sole can be placed in a frying pan without the potato scales moving around. Put the fish, scales down, in a non-stick frying pan over a medium heat and slowly sauté. Tilt the pan occasionally and use a spoon to pour the liquid in the pan over the sole. Carefully turn after 5 minutes and sauté for a further 5 minutes.

Serve immediately, garnished with lemon wedges and sprigs of flat-leaf parsley.

small bunch fresh sage

 bunch fresh parsley

 500 g/1 lb 2 oz small waxy potatoes

 4 sole

 salt

 1 lemon

 4 tbsp plain flour

 125 ml/4 fl oz sunflower oil

 100 g/3½ oz butter

Sole in Sage Butter

1. Take the sage leaves off their stalks. Chop the parsley. Peel the potatoes. Bring a saucepan of lightly salted water to the boil, add the potatoes, bring back to the boil and cook until tender. Slit the fish on both sides along the backbone. This makes it easier to remove the bones later. Season with salt and sprinkle some lemon juice over. Dust with flour, removing any excess. Heat an oval frying pan over a medium heat, add the oil, then add the fish and fry on the white-skinned side for 5 minutes, until golden brown. Turn and fry for a further 5 minutes. Spoon out the oil, add 80 g/2¾ oz of butter and allow it to foam.

2. Re-fry the fish in the butter, basting occasionally. Drain the potatoes. Add the remaining butter and the parsley to the potatoes and season to taste with salt.

3. Add the sage leaves to the pan and continue to pour butter over the sole until the sage leaves are crisp. Arrange the potatoes on serving plates. Place the whole fish on each plate and pour the sage butter over them.

Serve immediately with the parsley potatoes on the side.

■ The bones of a fried sole can be carefully removed with a spoon. Serve sole with fresh spinach or white wine sauce.

2 turbot, about 800 g/ 1 lb 12 oz each

 salt and white pepper

 30 g/1 oz plain flour

 4 tbsp vegetable oil

 60 g/2¼ oz butter

 ½ bunch fresh parsley

 juice of 1 lemon

(1)

Turbot Fillet Fried on the Bone

1. Fillet the turbot along the backbone. Season both sides of the turbot fillets with salt and pepper and lightly dust with flour. Remove any excess flour. Heat the oil in a large frying pan. Add the turbot and fry for 5 minutes on the dark-skinned side, continually basting the fish with oil from the pan. Turn and fry on the other side for a further 5 minutes.

2. Remove the oil from the pan, add the butter and slowly sauté the turbot over a low heat for 2 minutes, ensuring that the butter doesn't get too brown.

3. While the turbot is still in the pan, remove the dark skin. It will be easy to remove from the cooked fish. Season to taste with salt.

4. Chop the parsley and add to the pan with the lemon juice. Slightly tilt the pan and continue to baste butter from the pan over the turbot.

Place the fish on serving plates, pour over the parsley butter and serve immediately.

■ As an alternative, you can prepare one 300 g/10½ oz turbot fillet per person. Tarragon, basil and chives can be substituted for the parsley.

250 g/9 oz sardines

2 tbsp flour

2 litres/3½ pints vegetable oil, for frying

salt

lemon wedges, to serve

①

Fried Sardines

1. Clean the sardines under cold running water. Slowly break away the head towards the top, pulling out the innards at the same time.

2. Open the stomach with your thumb and wash it thoroughly. After removing the head you can loosen the backbone and remove it completely, if wished.

3. Place the sardines or sardine fillets in a sieve, pat dry and sprinkle with the flour.

4. Hold the sieve over the sink and shake off any excess flour.

5. Put the oil into a wide saucepan and heat to 170°C/340°F. Add the sardines and fry for 2 minutes for whole sardines, 1 minute for fillets. Remove from the oil and drain on kitchen paper. Season with salt.

Serve immediately with lemon wedges.

15

■ 'Italian-style' sardines are marinated in balsamic vinegar and olive oil and served cold with white bread.

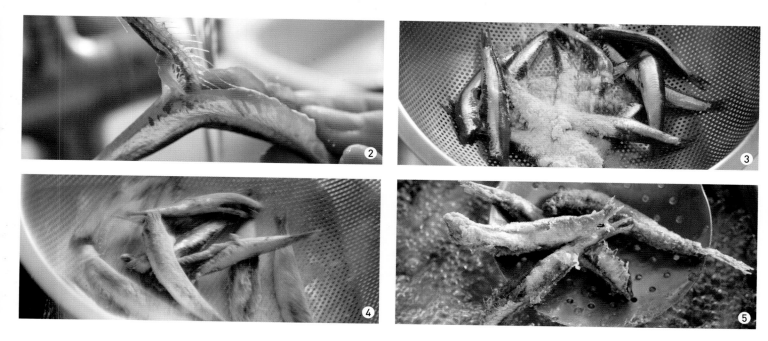

8 garlic cloves

 small bunch fresh parsley

 2 dried jalapeño chillies

 1 kg/2 lb 4 oz raw king prawns

 150 ml/5 fl oz extra virgin olive oil

 coarse sea salt

 a few drops of lemon juice

(1)

Garlic Prawns

1. Peel the garlic and thinly slice. Chop the parsley. Lightly press down on the chillies. Peel the prawns.

2. Heat the oil in a frying pan over a medium heat, add the chillies and the garlic and cook until lightly browned.

3. After about 1 minute add the prawns and sauté for a further 2 minutes. Add the parsley and season to taste with salt and a few drops of lemon juice.

Serve immediately with fresh white bread or cooked rice.

■ Mix some chopped spaghetti and a few tomato cubes into the garlic prawns. Add a few spoons of cooking water, so that the oil binds better with the pasta.

1 small pineapple

 500 g/1 lb 2 oz cooked prawns

 300 ml/10 fl oz Cocktail Sauce
(see below)

 4 orange slices

 4 celery leaves

Prawn Cocktail with Cocktail Sauce

1. Cut off the pineapple skin with a knife.

2. Cut the pineapple into quarters lengthways and cut out the core and any remaining brown 'eyes'.

3. Cut the pineapple in 5-mm/¼-inch cubes, about the size of the prawns.

4. Place the prawns and the pineapple in a bowl, add the cocktail sauce and mix.

Serve in small bowls, garnished with orange slices and some celery leaves.

■ To make Cocktail Sauce, add 3 tablespoons of tomato ketchup, 2 teaspoons of grated horseradish, 3 tablespoons of cognac and the juice of ½ an orange to 200 ml/7 fl oz of mayonnaise. Blend with a whisk until smooth. Add a pinch of salt, a pinch of cayenne pepper and 3 drops of Worcestershire sauce.

8 scallops

 8 bacon rashers

 1 tbsp vegetable oil

 salt and pepper

 8 tbsp coarse sea salt, to serve

Fried Scallops Wrapped in Bacon

1. Remove the white flesh from the scallop shells. Clean the bottom shell, remove any remaining parts of the corals and reserve. Dry the shells and set aside until the dish is ready to serve.

2. Lay the bacon rashers on a work surface. Place the white scallop flesh on one end and roll up in the bacon.

3. Heat a little of the vegetable oil in a frying pan. Place the bacon-wrapped scallops in the pan and season to taste with pepper. Do not add salt, because the bacon provides plenty of flavour.

4. Pan-fry the scallops on both sides for about 1 minute until the bacon is crisp.

5. Place the reserved corals in a separate frying pan with the remaining oil and quickly fry on both sides. Season lightly with salt and pepper. Sprinkle the sea salt on small serving plates and arrange the shells firmly on it. Place the bacon-wrapped scallops in the shells.

Garnish with the fried corals and serve immediately.

■ This dish is served as a starter. However, the scallops can be fried without the bacon and served with asparagus salad or in pumpkin soup.

*
*
*
30

100 g/3½ oz fresh
white breadcrumbs

 300 g/10½ oz crabmeat

 small bunch fresh coriander

 2 tbsp crème fraîche

 3 eggs

 salt

 pepper

 2 tbsp vegetable oil

Crispy Crab Cakes

1. Put the crabmeat into a mixing bowl and crush with a fork so it will be easier to mix with the other ingredients.

2. Finely chop the coriander. Add the crème fraîche to the crabmeat. Separate 2 eggs and add the yolks to the crabmeat with the remaining whole egg. Season to taste with salt and pepper and mix in the coriander.

3. Add half the breadcrumbs and mix. Cover and chill in the refrigerator for 15 minutes. The mixture is easier to work with when cold.

4. Using a tablespoon, take some of the mixture from the bowl and shape into cakes by hand. Dip the crab cakes into the remaining breadcrumbs.

5. Heat the oil in a non-stick frying pan. Add the crab cakes and fry on both sides for 2–3 minutes until golden brown, turning them over carefully.

Arrange the crab cakes on plates and serve with a dip.

■ **Dip recommendation:** Pour 200 ml/7 fl oz of tomato ketchup into a mixing bowl, add 1 teaspoon of finely grated fresh ginger and mix in a few drops of Tabasco sauce. The cakes can also be prepared with raw, chopped prawns or with leftovers of other cooked shellfish instead of the crabmeat.

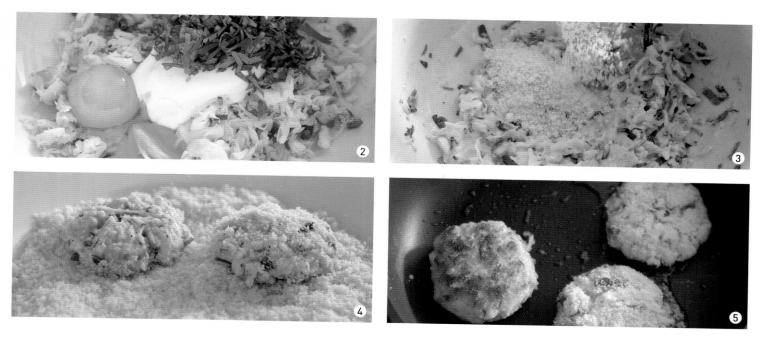

2 kg/4 lb 8 oz live crayfish

 3 carrots

 3 spring onions

 3 shallots

 2 leeks

 4 celery sticks

 1 garlic clove

 large bunch fresh dill

 5 cloves

 1 tsp black peppercorns

 3 bay leaves

 1 dried jalapeño chilli

 500 ml/18 fl oz white wine

 2 tbsp coarse sea salt

 150 ml/5 fl oz mayonnaise and lightly toasted white bread, to serve

Crayfish in Dill Stock

1. First check that the crayfish are still moving; if not, discard them. Peel the carrots, spring onions and shallots. Cut the leeks in half. Cut the celery and the other vegetables into 5-mm/¼-inch slices. Crush the garlic clove in its skin. Chop the dill, reserving a few sprigs to garnish.

2. Pour 5 litres/8½ pints of water into a large saucepan with the cloves, peppercorns, bay leaves, chilli, wine and salt and bring to the boil. Add the vegetables and the dill and simmer for 3 minutes.

3. Place half of the crayfish in the simmering stock. Cover with a lid and immediately bring back to the boil. When the crayfish have turned red, remove them with a large skimming ladle. Add the remaining crayfish and cook.

Break away the tails and arrange the crayfish on a plate with a little mayonnaise and the reserved dill sprigs. Serve with lightly toasted white bread.

■ Serve the crayfish in a large bowl placed in the centre of the table, so that everyone can help themselves. Savour the crayfish during the summer months with a fresh white wine and some Cocktail Sauce (see page 44).

40

4 corn cobs

 4 lobsters

 coarse sea salt

 cayenne pepper

 100 g/3½ oz butter

fine sea salt

Boiled Lobster with Sweetcorn & Melted Butter

1. Remove the leaves and silks from the corn cobs, and cut off the stalks. Add water to a saucepan large enough to hold all the corn cobs and bring to the boil. Do not add any salt to the water – it could make the corn tough.

2. Place the corn in the boiling water and simmer for 8 minutes.

3. Using a knife, remove the elastic bands from the lobster pincers. Fill a separate saucepan with 5 litres/8½ pints of water and bring to the boil. Season to taste with some coarse sea salt and cayenne pepper.

4. Put the lobster into the boiling water head-first and bring the water back to the boil. Reduce the heat and simmer for 10 minutes.

5. Melt the butter in a small saucepan. Arrange the lobster on four serving plates. Add one corn cob to each plate, drizzle with the melted butter and sprinkle with some fine sea salt.

Serve immediately, with lobster pliers to crack open the lobster.

■ There are many companies that will deliver fresh lobster to your door.

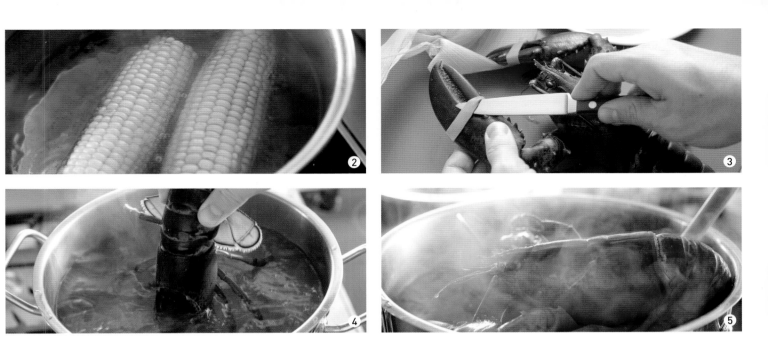

3 shallots

 60 g/2¼ oz celery

 1 leek

 1 garlic clove

 30 g/1 oz butter

 2 bay leaves

 1 fresh thyme sprig

 salt and pepper

 2 kg/4 lb 8 oz live mussels, scrubbed and debearded

 150 ml/5 fl oz white wine

 ½ bunch fresh parsley, finely chopped

Mussels Steamed in White Wine

1. Peel the shallots and cut into fine strips. Slice the celery and leek into fine strips. Press the garlic clove in its skin. Melt the butter in a saucepan. Add the garlic and shallots, then add the bay leaves, thyme, celery and leek, and sauté briefly. Season to taste with salt and pepper.

2. Add the mussels and mix with the vegetables. Pour in the wine, cover the pan and leave to simmer for 3–5 minutes until the mussels open. Sprinkle the parsley over the mussels.

Mix well and serve immediately.

■ Use an empty mussel shell to eat the cooked mussels without cutlery.

2 tomatoes

2 shallots

5 fresh basil leaves

bunch fresh parsley

salt and pepper

3 tbsp red wine vinegar

8 tbsp olive oil

2 kg/4 lb 8 oz cooked mussels

Mussels Served Cold in a Herb Marinade

1. Peel the tomatoes, cut them into quarters and deseed and dice. Dice the shallots. Chop the basil leaves and the parsley, then combine everything in a small mixing bowl.

2. Season to taste with salt and pepper and pour over the vinegar. Add the oil and mix well.

3. Remove the cooked mussels from their shells. Place the mussels in the herb marinade, cover with clingfilm and chill in the refrigerator for 30 minutes.

Arrange the mussels in bowls and serve with toasted white bread.

 ✳ ✳ ✳ **60**

■ This dish is especially delicious made with cockles, clams or cooked whelks. It is particularly important not to serve them directly from the refrigerator, but at room temperature.

2

3

2 garlic cloves

 bunch fresh parsley

 8 cuttlefish

 salt and pepper

 1 fresh rosemary sprig, plus extra sprigs to garnish

 pinch of dried chilli flakes

 4 tbsp extra virgin olive oil

 300 g/10½ oz natural yogurt

 1 lemon

Grilled Cuttlefish

1. Peel and chop the garlic. Finely chop the parsley. Clean the cuttlefish thoroughly and dry with kitchen paper. Place on a work surface, smooth side up, and make shallow slits across its width.

2. Place in a soufflé dish with the slit side on top, season with salt and pepper on the inside, fill with the parsley and half the garlic and turn over.

3. Pluck the rosemary off the stalk, combine with the chilli flakes, and spread over the cuttlefish. Season again with salt and pepper and sprinkle 2 tablespoons of the oil over. Marinate for 15 minutes. You can also marinate the cuttlefish the day before cooking this dish.

4. Heat a non-stick frying pan, add the cuttlefish and sear, slit side first, then turn. Cook for about 2–3 minutes on each side.

5. Put the yogurt, the remaining garlic and the remaining oil in a mixing bowl. Season to taste with salt and pepper and mix.

Slice the lemon and arrange with the cuttlefish on serving plates. Garnish with rosemary sprigs and serve with the yogurt and garlic dip.

■ You can also use fresh squid for this dish. Cuttlefish and squid taste even more delicious when chargrilled and served with tomato vinaigrette and fresh white bread.

1 kg/2 lb 4 oz octopus

 2 tbsp coarse sea salt

 1 lemon, halved, and 1 half sliced

 1 fresh thyme sprig

 250 ml/9 fl oz white wine

 1 tbsp sweet paprika

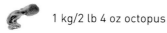 ¼ tsp cayenne pepper

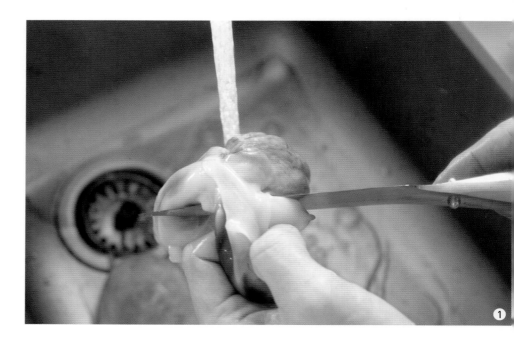 4 tbsp extra virgin olive oil

Cooked Octopus with Lukewarm Vinaigrette

1. Thoroughly wash the octopus. Turn the body inside out, pull away the entrails and cut them off with a knife.

2. Rinse thoroughly and remove any remaining skin.

3. Pinch the lower part of the head of the octopus in order to grip the beak and remove it.

4. Bring a deep saucepan of water to the boil, then place the octopus in it with the salt, lemon slices and thyme.

5. Simmer for about 40 minutes. Cut a piece from the octopus and taste it to check that it is cooked. To make the vinaigrette, pour the juice of half the lemon into a mixing bowl. Add the wine, paprika and cayenne pepper. Mix with the oil and 1 tablespoon of the hot cooking liquid from the octopus. Remove the octopus from the pan, drain and slice.

Arrange on serving plates, sprinkle with the vinaigrette and serve immediately.

■ In Spain, cooked octopus is often served on cooked potato slices. It is also delicious when served with fresh garlic sauce or on a mixed bean salad. The cooking time depends largely on the size of the octopus. This is why it should be tasted to check that it is tender.

70

1 shallot

5 tbsp red wine vinegar

1 tbsp water

24 oysters

Oysters on Ice

1. Peel the shallot and finely chop. Pour the vinegar into a bowl with the water, add the chopped shallot and mix.

2. Crack the oysters with an oyster knife.

3. Open the oysters and serve on a platter with crushed ice. Place the sauce in a small bowl in the centre of the platter.

■ Rock oysters such as Fines de Claires, Portugaise, Sylter Spezial or the American Blue Point are true delicacies when eaten raw.

30

 24 oysters

 2 leeks

 2 tsp butter

 salt and pepper

 freshly grated nutmeg

 200 ml/7 fl oz Hollandaise sauce

 1 kg/2 lb 4 oz coarse sea salt

Baked Oysters

1. Open the oysters, remove from their shells and place in a sieve. Clean the oyster shells and place in a preheated low oven for 3–5 minutes to dry. Wash the leeks and slice diagonally into fine strips.

2. Heat the butter in a saucepan until foaming. Add the leeks, season to taste with salt and pepper and nutmeg, and cook until brown. Add 100 ml/3½ fl oz of water and simmer for 2–3 minutes until the leeks are cooked and the liquid is reduced. Place the leeks in the oyster shells and put the oysters on top.

3. Meanwhile, preheat the grill to medium. Pour the Hollandaise sauce over the oysters and cook for 2–3 minutes under the preheated grill. Make sure that the oysters do not turn brown.

Spread a thick layer of sea salt over the base of a large platter, then put the oysters on top and serve.

■ **Oysters removed from their shells can be baked like fried fish in a beer batter and served with tartare sauce, or fried wrapped in bacon and served on sauerkraut.**

45

INDEX